Contents

Acknowledgements

I would like to thank the people who made this book possible. The first is my brother in law, Ross Woodstock. Six years ago when I tried to put some thoughts together about joy, Ross communicated to me that it was a wonderful idea. This summer when I got serious about writing he was most encouraging even as he made corrections.

Then a friend John Murphy encouraged me with statements like:

- well organized
- written simply
- great use of illustrations
- pathway to joy is very clear

Rev. Mike Hixon spent a lot of time going over every sentence to save me a lot of embarrassment.

Plus, a great big thank you to my wife Beverly. She did all my typing. Even more than typing, however; she kept me encouraged when I considered this project to be way beyond my ability. I love being married to this woman.

Finally, my appreciation goes out to friends:

> Colleen Sheedlo
> Celia Woodworth
> Pastor Wes Coffey
> Pastor Glen Pettigrove
> James McKay
> Jon Roberts
> Barbara MacDonald Nelson
> Rev. Ron McClung

Dedication

I am very pleased to dedicate this book to my children and their spouses:

Shalin & David White

Bradley & Sarah Emerson

John & Brooke Emerson

I am even more serious in dedicating it to my six grandchildren, because they are entering into a world that is far different from one in which I was raised. They will be tempted by a media that goes one step further every year just to get a better rating. Their programming will include more killings, rapes, and sensuous living than I was ever exposed to. They will be persuaded by brilliant advertising agencies that are bent on changing their minds no matter what their parents have taught them. To my beautiful grandchildren:

> Jake White
> Hawken White
> Ethan Emerson
> Lily Emerson
> Porter Emerson
> Mitchell Emerson

may you read this and understand that no matter how the world tries to sway you, there is a journey of joyful living that can only be found in one Book - - - a book that has been a pleasing guide to my life and a book that will never deceive you just to become more popular.

It is my prayer that you discover your "Hidden Treasure" and that you will always remember how much you are loved.

Introduction

In Plain Sight?

Ever have trouble finding something? I usually have no trouble in a hardware store. The clerks seem to stand at the door and fight over the customers, but in a grocery store I am lost. There have to be at least five million items in each aisle, so when my wife asks me to pick something up I know I am in for a long hunt. One day she asked me to bring home some peanut butter, a staple in our home. I searched every single aisle including the deli, cookie, ice cream and even donut aisle (I once had a peanut butter donut) and found nothing that resembled peanut butter. Either they were out of peanut butter, or they saw me coming and hid every jar in the back of the store.

Finally, I found someone who worked in the store and asked my standard question, "If you worked here where would you hide the peanut butter?" With a smile she said, "Follow me." I then added that if this was my store I would stock the peanut butter next to the jelly, since they always go together. She led me down an aisle, and there was the peanut butter, eye level, right next to the jelly. I'm not sure why I couldn't find it by myself. Maybe I was so frustrated that I walked up and down the aisles with my eyes closed - - - I don't know.

Have you ever had trouble finding something in plain sight? Perhaps you misplaced something in your home, and after searching a whole day, found it right where it should be located. A neighbor lady called a friend complaining that she couldn't find her cell phone. The friend asked her what she was using to call her. One day I could not find my coat. Finally I asked my wife if she knew where it was, and she said she hung it up in the closet. My response, "Well, that is a dumb place to hide it."

Joy can be harder to discover in life than peanut butter in a grocery store. It's in plain sight, and yet it's hidden because we look for it in all the wrong places. We all want to be joyful and live a fulfilling life. However, most people have trouble understanding joy and so are willing to only settle for moments of happiness. The difference between joy and happiness is that joy is with you no matter what is happening around you while happiness is fully dependent on what is happening around you. If moments of happiness are all you have to look forward to, then you have to tolerate moments of sadness; because happiness and sadness are on the same emotional level.

Happiness comes when nice things happen to you. The excitement about buying a new car brings a moment of happiness. There is the hunt for the model that fits your lifestyle and makes a statement, the excitement of trying to read the instrumentation, and that wonderful smell. You are not even worried about the interest rates and financing, because your emotions are momentarily filled with excitement.

Possibly your happiness comes from a much deserved promotion at work. Maybe it means more money, or more prestige, or even more travel. Your neighbors congratulate you because it is long overdue and your spouse is thrilled.

Happy moments come when you meet the perfect lifemate, walk the aisle or witness the birth of your first child. It may come when you purchase your first home.

The emotions of happiness come because pleasant things happen to you. But if that is your greatest level of pleasure on this earth then you also have to be content with happenings that make you sad. This sadness may come when a child makes a decision that you know will hurt them (because it hurt you thirty-five years earlier). Sadness and hurt may come when you receive divorce papers unexpectedly, or watch as a loved one grows weaker and weaker and then passes away. Along with many happy moments in this life you will also witness many sad moments. So if your only goal in life is to experience a few happy moments, then you also have to put up with a lot of sad moments.

Happiness and sadness both deal with your emotions at the same level. There is a reality in your life, however, that is far greater than happiness and sadness and that reality is JOY. JOY is a hidden treasure very few people know about, and even fewer discover. It is a hidden treasure in plain sight. This book is written to help you move beyond the emotional roller coaster ride of happy moments and sad moments. It is a simple book, but then the pathway to joy is simple - - - hidden but simple.

You will discover the best part of joy is that it does not come with a negative counterpart like sadness. Joy stands by itself, far above any other emotion. That means you can experience joy even in the saddest of times.

Are you ready for a wonderful journey to discover joy for your life? Then you will enjoy what you are about to read.

Chapter # 1

My Personal Treasure Hunt

It was the most embarrassing day of my life. That wonderful smell of burning leaves filled the air and the temperature was about sixty degrees. It was a perfect night to play football. Hopefully the weather for next week's homecoming game would turn out this beautiful.

As we left the locker room to play the second half of the game, a limousine was circling the field. It was an old rusty limousine and had probably seen many funerals in its day, as funeral homes were the only businesses that owned limousines in our small town.

The limousine pulled up in front of the grandstand, stopped, and a gangly 6'2" hairy legged guy stepped out in a strapless evening gown escorted by the shortest guy in the senior class. The audience roared in laughter as the Varsity Club used this stunt to promote next week's homecoming.

When the crowd regained control of their senses, an emcee interviewed the 6'2" raving beauty. This guy/girl talked with a farm drawl and thanked God he got the milking done in time to be there. He also said he had put on a lot of "Old Spice" to overpower any smell of cow he might have brought with him.

It was funny, yes even hilarious, but it was the most embarrassing day of my life because that rusty old limousine was our family car. I knew the audience was laughing at the mock homecoming queen, but I also realized that our family car added to the humor. Why did our family have to be made a spectacle of in front of the whole community?

14

Everyone knew that was our car. Why did my dad go out and purchase this conspicuous, ugly old car that was so different from every other family car in our community? Why couldn't we drive a Chevy or a Ford station wagon like everyone else? I didn't care about owning an expensive car. I just wanted a car like other families so I could fit in.

I knew the answers in my heart. Dad purchased that eleven year old DeSoto limousine because it was cheap and it held all eight family members. But, why did we have to display our low income in front of the whole community that evening, and from my perspective, why did the people in the grandstand need to laugh at my family?

Those were the days when young men let their testosterone show by giving their muscle cars names like "Temptation" or "The Beast". The names were usually decoratively painted on the back fenders of their cars. So after that night of embarrassment it didn't take my brother and me long to name the limousine. We had to do something to regain a little dignity, and laughing at ourselves was one way of doing so.

Across both back fenders we painted the name "The Last Ride". It wasn't a name used on many muscle cars and we didn't exactly feel a testosterone rush when we did it but it seemed to fit what our family car had previously been used for - - - funerals. My mother scolded both of us for our antics and I don't remember her ever driving the car to town again. Dad, however, thought it was very clever and revealed that he was proud of his two sons.

The name was in place, and my classmates thought it was funny. It was my way of neutralizing the embarrassment. By painting a humorous name on the back of that car I was declaring that our family was humorous, not poor.

Journey to Overcome

That evening started me on a fifteen year journey to overcome my embarrassment. It was a journey to become successful, earn a lot of money, and buy a car that would dazzle the community instead of a car that would be laughed at. At sixteen I'm not sure I defined my path in that manner; but I knew I never wanted to be laughed at by the whole community ever again.

By the age of twenty eight I had landed a wonderful sales job with adidas athletic shoes, and I did begin to earn more money than I ever dreamed I could earn. That set me on a quest to buy expensive cars. I was not going to embarrass my family in the way my father had embarrassed me.

My first purchase was a brand new 1973 Olds 98 with a 455 cubic inch engine. That car was beautiful. It didn't settle down to cruising speed until about 85 mph. (I'm not saying I ever drove that fast, however.) It took two K Mart parking lots just to park it. When I parked it in front of a customer's store that had angle parking, I was afraid I would get a ticket for blocking one lane of traffic. My next three cars were all Mercedes. The first one was used, but it was a beautiful car. The second one was brand new, but it came with a huge car payment that was twice my mortgage payment. It was a beautiful bright orange, plus I had a mobile telephone installed, which was very prestigious (way before cell phones).

My third Mercedes was brand new and I was able to pay cash for it. In my mind I had arrived. I had reached the end of my journey. I had accomplished what I had set out to accomplish. Now I could coast the rest of the way through life. The embarrassment of that mock homecoming fifteen years earlier was now set to rest. No one was laughing at me now. In fact I sensed admiration (or jealousy) in the eyes of my neighbors and friends.

I was very happy and pleased with myself as I drove the Mercedes around the state calling on customers, but I began to realize that a moment of happiness did not spell out a life filled with joy. That third Mercedes was only about a week old when I began to realize it was not the answer I was looking for. It made me feel I had arrived, but I still felt there had to be more to life than a fancy car. Something was still missing.

It was like I had one small part of my life in order, but I realized there were so many other parts of my life that could fall apart. I was also a little arrogant because of my success, when the owner of one of my larger accounts threatened me with an awful thought. He said, "You had better be kind to people on the way up the ladder of success, because you are going to have to face them again on the way down." I thought, "You

19

mean my wonderful success may not last forever? You mean I could lose my job and drive my children around in an embarrassing old car some day?"

There Had To Be More To Life

I was happy for the moment but not joyful. Surely there was more to life than being successful in business and owning an expensive car. I knew I could lose my job, and I knew that my expensive car would get rusty and even start using oil in the next ten years. I realized that my Mercedes was four thousand pounds of cold steel, hard plastic, and rather smelly diesel fuel. It did not have feelings for me, love me, or even care about me.

Even more unsettling was the fact that I began to run through my mind future purchases that would bring me to the same conclusion. Possibly a cottage on a lake in northern Michigan would fulfill my need for lasting happiness. Perhaps that would end my journey and even make me joyful. What about buying a sailboat or even a beautiful customized van? Maybe I should learn to fly and buy my own airplane, or better yet, hire a pilot to jet me around the countryside.

As I went through scenario after scenario I always ended with the same conclusion. These would give me momentary happiness, but not fulfillment, and not a continual joy in my heart. Was my journey over? Is that all there was to life? Was a moment of happiness here and there all life had to offer? Was my journey through life to only consist of moments of pleasure intertwined with periods of dissatisfaction?

I really wanted more. In fact I really needed more in order to go on. I was not suicidal or even depressed, but I needed more out of life than just a beautiful car and a successful job. I needed a feeling of completion in my life, a feeling that I had finally arrived.

It was about that time I remembered a Bible verse I had learned as a child. It said,

> *"Do not store up for yourself treasures on earth, where moth and rust destroy, and where thieves break in and steal. But store up for yourselves treasures in heaven, where moth and rust do not destroy, and where thieves do not break in and steal. --- " Matt. 6:19-20*

That was a wonderful eureka moment in my life. I realized I was gauging all my happiness by earthly treasure that could not possibly bring me the complete life I was looking for. So without even stopping my brand new Mercedes, I did something I absolutely did not want to do. I did not want to become a religious person, and I did not want to be governed by a bunch of rules that would take all the fun out of my life, but I knew what the next step had to be. I struck a deal with God that would leave me a way out if this failed to bring meaning to my life.

I asked God to forgive my sins and asked Jesus to be Lord of my life. I told God I would follow Him for six months in a quiet sort of way, and then either opt to stay with Him or walk away if that, also, proved fruitless. It was a commitment, and I was serious; but I did not want to flaunt this commitment before anyone in case I had to back out.

I don't know the mechanics of what happened next, but my life was almost instantly different. There was an amazing peace that entered my life. It was like a deep inner peace that I had never experienced before. It was like I no longer disagreed with God or even argued against God's Word as a method of excusing my lifestyle. I was now on His team, agreeing with His ways. I was now on God's team and somehow began to look forward to all the future held for me. I had discovered a contentment and a deep inner peace in my life.

23

My Life Began To Change

My sales began to climb over the next six months because I began to see my customers as partners in business rather than a pay check. I was there to help them and not just use them. Gradually my wife became more beautiful to me even though I felt our marriage was falling apart. My children became more important to me and were more fun to be with. Gradually peanut butter even tasted better, if that were possible. People slowly began to ask what was different about me.

That peace became even more evident as time went on. My wife was pregnant with our third child, John Calvin, and in the week she was supposed to deliver I had to fly to Germany for a business meeting. I was worried, because as a man, I knew she could not deliver this child without me by her side. So as I sat in that Lufthansa 747, I prayed and asked God why I had to be gone during such an important event?

In a few minutes a peace came over me and I was able to comfortably settle down into my seat. It was like God was saying, "First of all, she can deliver without you, and second, you will be there to witness the birth of your son." I flew to Germany and the meetings finished earlier than expected. I changed my flight home to arrive a day early. As I walked into the house I said, "Honey, I'm home."And she said, "Not for long you aren't. Where have you been? Don't you know I have been trying to have this baby all day?" We went straight to the hospital and John Calvin was born within the hour. What a wonderful gift from God.

I had discovered something called JOY and it was beautiful. It filled my heart during my happy times as well as my sad times. It was something I had never experienced before and I was bent on keeping it. A year later I remembered the six month commitment I had made with God. Whether it meant obeying rules or not, there was not even a hint of wanting to go back to my old life. I was ready to continue on this path for the rest of my life. The reward was far too great to let it go. It was a deep inner peace and that brought joy to my heart.

I would guess that no one reading this book has traveled the same journey I have traveled only to discover an emptiness upon arrival. Cars may not be as important to you as they were to me, because you never had to drive your date to a prom in something called "The Last Ride." Plus you never had to experience a whole community laughing at you because of the vehicle your family drove.

Many of you have experienced other journeys that left you less than satisfied with life. Perhaps your education was one of your uppermost goals. Then, after one or two PhD's you still didn't feel you had arrived.

26

Maybe owning your own business was a part of your journey only to discover it took up a lot of your time and the problems you had to solve on a daily basis took a lot of happiness out of your life.

Many men and women focus on an intense career to find a completion in life only to discover the wear and tear on the body isn't worth it. The loss of your family can be heart wrenching because of the intensity of your work schedule. Some look forward to retirement and travel only to discover that one day just slips into the next. The loss of the feeling of being needed can leave you empty.

We all seem to be searching for self worth, a need to be needed and respected. We are just on different journeys to get there. Whatever the journey may be, the results will almost always be the same . . . our journey is complete but we still feel a need to get more out of life. We desire a joy that will never leave us. We desire more than the roller coaster ride of happiness and sadness and happiness and sadness.

Wouldn't it be wonderful if we could discover that joy? Is joy even possible? I'm here to tell you it is. It just looks a whole lot different than we think. It is hidden, but, in plain sight.

Chapter #2
Is There A Treasure?

My two grandsons wanted to show me an old abandoned gold mine high in the Sierra Mountains near Bishop, California. A lot of gold had been mined from that area years earlier but it is mined out by now. The adventure turned out to be a little less than spectacular, because there was not even a hint of gold in the mine and the mine shaft was only about 5' 6" tall. We walked about fifty yards into the mine shaft and the only excitement was to sign an "I've Been Here" guest book at the end of the tunnel. The hike was beautiful, however, and the time with my grandsons was precious. The

Sierra mountains are beautiful, even at eight thousand feet where the air gets a little thin.

On the way back to the cabin we crossed a small moutain stream of crystal clear water, and as I looked down, admiring the beauty of God's creation, I was almost blinded by the shimmer of gold at the bottom of the stream. Apparently the sun was shining at the correct angle now and the crystal clear water just magnified the intensity of the gold. The beauty was almost blinding.

My first thought was to keep moving and not say a word. I was going to become rich. I was going to sell everything I owned including a couple children, go to the proper authorities, and buy the whole mountain. I would then begin the mining process and become rich. I could finally belong to a country club and even buy brand new golf clubs for the first time in my life. But that whole thought process lasted perhaps one or two seconds because I knew many people had traveled that well worn path, and as yet, none had begun the mining process.

It Was "Fool's Gold"

I was looking at iron pyrite which is called "Fool's Gold". I will have to admit that the angle of the sun and the crystal clear mountain stream made that "Fools Gold" a beautiful and blinding sight. Just to be sure, however, I scooped up a handful and took it back to the cabin to dry out. Sure enough the brilliance I had witnessed earlier was not the same.

Is there a treasure? What if the joy I am talking about is only "Fool's Gold?" What if the joy I am talking about is only programming my mind to think more positive? Is there really a joy we can discover as we walk on this earth? What if a beautiful moment in our life excites us so much that we think we are experiencing joy, but then a few weeks later

31

it becomes less and less brilliant? What if we never experience real joy but only moments of happiness and sadness? What if we only have moments of experiencing the beauty of iron pyrite in that beautiful mountain stream, which turns out to be less than fulfilling or even disappointing in the long run?

"Is There A Treasure?" Is there something out there that will bring me joy during the happy times of my life as well as the sad times? Or, am I going to spend the rest of my life seeking one adventure after another, only to discover there is nothing that will bring me fulfillment? What if I tell you that God has laid out a recipe for achieving joy in your life? Would you be willing to follow His directions?

To see if there is a treasure called joy, I'm going to look into a book that has proven itself reliable for centuries. It is a book referred to as the Bible and it not only declares that God desires for you to experience joy on this earth, but it also reveals the steps to discover it. Please don't short change yourself and stop reading here. To some the Bible is repulsive. Admittedly, some preachers and even angry church members have used the Bible as a "ball bat" to force Christians into submission. It has also been used to make people feel like second rate citizens. Whether the Bible is offensive to you or a daily reference book; it has proven itself to be very accurate in dealing with human nature and human emotions.

Isn't The Bible Just A Book Of Rules?

What does the Bible say about joy? I always thought the Bible was just a book about rules and regulations and a book that was very condemning. But, could there possibly be a softer side of God, a side where He wants to pour out blessings on the people He created? Could He possibly want His people to walk in laughter and joy while on this earth? Let's look.

The Bible talks about joy in a number of places, but, my favorite passage is in the gospel of John. In that book Jesus makes it very clear that God wants us to walk in an emotional state of complete joy as we walk on this earth. In John 15:10-11 Jesus states:

"If you obey My commands you will remain in My love, just as I have obeyed My Father's commands and remain in His love. I have told you this so that My joy may be in you and that your joy may be complete." (underling added)

Jesus, Himself, God's own Son, states without hesitation that His desire is for us to experience complete joy as we walk on this earth - - - complete joy even as we live in a less than perfect world. So, either Jesus knows that this is possible and we can actually experience it, or He is bent on deceiving us and lying to us. I don't know about you but I really hesitate to call Jesus a liar.

Joy For The Rest Of My Life

Jesus states that He wants us to have complete joy; not partial joy or momentary joy. He wants us to experience joy in the morning and joy all day long - - - joy in the evening and all night long, joy this week and next week and next year - - - complete joy for the rest of our lives. Not moments of emotional unstable highs followed by seasons of depression, but joy in our hearts for the rest of our lives - - - joy even when we experience difficulties in our life. So yes, there is a treasure.

King David, one of the greatest kings on the face of this earth, knew that same joy. Speaking to God he said:

"You have filled my heart with greater joy than when their grain and new wine abound." Psalm 4:7

Harvest time for the Hebrews and other ancient people were times of great celebration, rejoicing, and dancing. It was a time to be thankful for an abundance of grain and grapes; for without that harvest there would be hunger and hardship (food stamps had not yet been invented). Yet King David is saying that in God's presence he experiences greater joy than when the harvest is plentiful.

King David had experienced a state of joy and according to him it was more beautiful than any wonderful thing he had ever experienced on this earth. In Psalm 16:11 he once again brings up the subject of joy. Talking to God he states:

"You have made known to me the path of life; you will fill me with joy in your presence, with eternal pleasures at your right hand."

David knew this joy and found it in the presence of God and not in an abundance of earthly treasures. He discovered a joy by just being around God and listening to His directions, rather than going out and buying brand new chariots with chrome plated bumpers and CD players.

So we see that Jesus desires for us to experience joy and that King David had experienced joy. One of the most "joy filled" books in the Bible is Philippians. The Apostle Paul wrote this book under some very trying circumstances - - - circumstances that should have robbed him of all his joy and even moments of happiness. Circumstances that would make most of us cry out to God and say, "Why me, God? Where are you God?" You see, Paul wrote this book while in a Roman prison chained between two battle hardened Roman soldiers. Yet the theme of the book is "joy."

Can you imagine being chained between two Roman guards for twenty four hours a day before deodorant had been invented? Yet Paul talks about the joy he is experiencing on a continual basis under these conditions. In the book of Philippians he states that he can tolerate these conditions because:

- *His citizenship is in heaven and not here on earth (earthly problems do not get him down).*
- *He knows that God is able to bring about many wonderful things through his situation in a Roman prison.*
- *He knows that God is able to take his less than exciting circumstances and work them into something pretty amazing and wonderful.*
- *He knows that through his imprison-ment the people in Philippi will see a greater God than before and grow in the spiritual realm.*
- *He has learned to rejoice in God's presence, because His mighty, powerful, gracious, and loving God is always with him.*

I could go on and on to prove there is a reality known as joy, but let it suffice for now to know that Jesus desires for us to experience "complete joy", and that King David experienced that wonderful joy. Let us also understand that joy can be experienced during the worst of times as the Apostle Paul proves to us in the book of Philippians.

So, yes, there is a treasure and it is far greater than fool's gold. It is greater than the experience I had crossing that mountain stream and thinking I had discovered tremendous earthly wealth. What does the treasure look like? What does complete joy look like? Here is where the definition of joy goes far beyond our understanding. Here is why it is a hidden treasure in plain sight.

JOY, A HIDDEN TREASURE

Chapter #3

What Does The Treasure Look Like?

When I think of a joyful person I think of a cheerleader. A cheerleader has to be energetic, upbeat, and very positive no matter what is going on around them. When I was a sophomore in high school a lot of guys from our grade were called up to play varsity football. This happened because there were only two seniors on the team and one of them quit half way through the season. So the whole team was made up of sophomores and juniors.

You guessed it - - - we had a terrible season. We did not win a single game. In fact the scores were so lopsided that they would not even print them in the yearbook. I do remember one score being sixty-three to six. It was like every play the opposing team ran was for a touchdown. The only moments of grace came when they had an incomplete pass.

Yet there were the cheerleaders on the sideline yelling - - - "Victory, victory is our cry, V I C T O R Y - - -." They were upbeat and positive no matter how badly we were losing. That is what many people think joy looks like - - - being upbeat, energetic, and positive even in the worst of situations. Like I just lost my job but I know a better one will come along. Or, my spouse just died, but I am still going to remain positive.

Joy is not maintaining a positive mental attitude when the world around you is crumbling. The joy I am talking about is not a "mind control" exercise. It is not saying the glass is half full when in reality it is half empty. Joy is not cheering at a high school football game when the scores are so lopsided they wouldn't even print them in the yearbook.

That is how the world may define joy, and that is why so many people will never discover it. The joy found in the Bible is much different than just a positive mental attitude. In Philippians 4:6-7 Paul writes:

"Do not be anxious about anything, but in everything, by prayer and petition, with thanksgiving present your requests to God. And the peace of God, which transcends all understanding will guard your hearts and your minds in Christ Jesus."

Joy Is A Deep Inner Peace

There is the joy that is in plain sight but hidden from most. That joy can be defined as a "deep inner peace" that comes when we trust God and know that He has our back.

43

It's a deep inner peace that transcends the troubles in the world. It is a tranquility that cannot be found anywhere in this world. Look at this verse for just a moment as I define this hidden joy.

It starts out, "Do not be anxious (do not worry) about anything - - - ." I would say that is a pretty bold statement - - - do not be anxious about anything. It says do not worry when you are fired from your job unexpectedly and your rent is due. Do not be anxious when you are told your child has a serious illness. Do not worry when your child is making bad decisions that could be life altering.

When these troubles come, immediately go to God in prayer and keep praying. Bring your concern before Him. Look to the creator of this universe for help. Pray to the God who created you to become the object of His love and know that He will answer your prayer. Sometimes He will answer today, sometimes He will answer next week. Sometimes He

44

will answer in a more beautiful way than you ever considered. Sometimes you won't even recognize His answer as the answer. Sometimes He may answer in the opposite way you prayed, but understand that His answer is always the best possible answer.

End Your Prayers With Thanksgiving

Then, to continue following this formula for a deep inner peace, end your prayers by thanking Him (pray with thanksgiving) for the answer He will bring. It's like you are saying, "I don't know how you are going to get me enough money to pay the rent or maybe you are going to cause me to lose my place for reasons I don't understand, but I praise you for your beautiful answer, whatever it may be."

Maybe you are praying for a child who is making some really bad decisions and you say to God, "You have not answered this prayer for two years now, but I know the answer will be beautiful so I thank you for the answer, even though I have yet to witness it." That is called praying with thanksgiving and that kind of praying is guaranteed to bring you a serenity. That kind of prayer will start you on your journey to joy.

I mentioned earlier that when I made that six month commitment to God, a wonderful peace just overwhelmed me. I couldn't explain it, but it was an overwhelming and relaxing experience. I knew I was now on God's side, and I was no longer arguing with the King of kings and Lord of lords. Now I agreed with Him. Now I looked at Him as a wonderful caring God who was going to guide me through this life.

Other Peace Giving References

Let me share with you some other passages from God's Word that bring me that same deep inner peace. The first is a verse that helps me see that I will never be good enough to go to heaven. That idea should trouble me and cause me deep anxiety but look what it says. Philippians 3:9 brings me a great comfort rather than stirring me up. It reads

> *"--- not having a righteousness of my own that comes from the law, but that which is through faith in Christ - - -."*

I Am A Spiritual Failure

I have tried many times to live up to the laws in God's Word and have failed over and over again. Every time I fail I know I have upset God and I know that He may even turn His back on me. If I fail ten times a day I may even begin to question if I am righteous enough to be called a Christian.

Yet look what Paul says in this

verse. He is saying that no amount of law keeping, discipline, religious effort, or self improvement, will make him good enough to stand before God. He has no righteousness of his own - - - he will never be good enough. But the righteousness that makes him good enough comes from God and is poured out upon us. II Corinthians 5:21 states it this way:

> *"God made Him (Jesus) who had no sin to be sin for us, so that in Him we might become the righteousness of God."*

It's true. By myself I will never be righteous enough to please God and enter heaven at the death of my body. Without the understanding of these two verses I will always feel like a spiritual failure. I will always be anxious because I know I will never be good enough to measure up. But with these verses I know my perfection is not what puts me in right standing with

God. It is my relationship with Jesus and obedience to Him that God looks at, and if that relationship is growing, then in His eyes I am righteous. Now that brings me a deep inner peace. Rather than always feeling like a spiritual failure I know, by faith in what God's Word says, that I am righteous.

Another verse that brings me a deep inner peace is John 3:16. It's a verse that reveals to me how deeply this all powerful God truly does love me.

"For God so loved the world (me) that He gave His one and only Son, that whoever believes in Him shall not perish but have eternal life."

God created man to be the object of His love. He simply had to have someone to love because God is love. As humans we always feel we have to earn someone's love. I had to buy my girl friend a whole lot of hot fudge sundaes before she accepted my marriage proposal. I had to make myself pleasing to her. But God created me in His own image so I could understand His love and love Him back. And to nail this love down He had His one and only Son die on the cross and pay the penalty for my sins so I could become righteous enough to enter into His presence.

Now that gives me a deep inner peace. On this earth I have to earn another person's love. I have to be kind to that person. But from day one, God did what needed to be done so He could pour out His love upon me. He really does love me and wants the very best for me.

I also mentioned in chapter one about the amazing peace that overwhelmed me when I made that six month commitment to God. The only thing I can attribute that to is that I was no longer fighting with God. I was no longer arguing with Him about what was right and wrong. At that moment I became one with God and agreed with Him. At that moment I allowed the all knowing God to become all knowing in my life. At that moment I was in total unity with God and that brought me a deep inner peace.

Eternal life is another promise from God's Word that brings me a deep inner peace. I know my life will end within the next thirty years. But I know I will live eternally with my Savior Jesus, bathed in the gentle and glowing warmth of His love. I know that in heaven I will never catch another cold, experience another flu, have another hip replacement or ever sense the displeasure of conflict, plus the peanut butter will be eye level in the first aisle I enter. So, even though I am involved in this world with its troubles, I know this life will not go on forever and I will spend my eternity in a perfect place with someone I love very much.

Even My Mistakes Will Be Turned Around

Sometimes things happen in my life that are troubling to me. Often I bring these things on myself by making wrong decisions but sometimes they just happen. In Romans 8:28 I read:

"And we know that in all things God works for the good of those who love Him, who have been called according to His purpose."

When I truly come to grips with this verse and understand that God can turn every circumstance around for my good, even if it hurts me or embarrasses me, then I have within me a deep inner peace.

Joy is defined in the Bible as a deep inner peace. It is not something you have to create but is something God gives when we call Jesus our Savior and find great delight in His presence. Joy is then poured out upon us.

52

It is not a commodity you can buy in a nearby grocery store (found in the detergent aisle).

What is the pathway to joy? Is there a treasure map? Again, it is spelled out very clearly. It is in plain sight - - - hidden, but in plain sight.

JOY, A HIDDEN TREASURE

Chapter # 4

The Treasure Map

Is there really a treasure map to a life of complete joy, or do I just have to experiment with life to discover joy? I would sure hate to go on another fifteen year journey only to discover I was, once again, on the wrong path. The answer is simple. Yes, there is a treasure map, and it is very simple and clear to follow.

Jesus said in the Gospel of John that He wanted us to experience His joy which in turn would give us complete joy. But, with every promise in God's Word ("that my joy may be in you and your joy may be complete") there comes a condition we must meet to receive the promise. That condition becomes our treasure map. So what is the condition that we must meet to find complete joy? What is the map?

Jesus said in John 15:10-11,

"If you obey my commands, you will remain in my love, just as I have obeyed my Father's commands and remain in His love. I have told you this so that my joy may be in you and your joy may be complete."

The condition we must meet if we want complete joy on this earth is to obey His commandments. The treasure map is simply to obey the commands Jesus has given us. Many will say, "There are those burdensome commands again. There are those strict rules and regulations that keep so many people away from God." But Jesus says that to have

complete joy we must knuckle under - - - obey
- - - give in to a very strict way of living.

I mentioned earlier in the book that
when I realized my Mercedes was nice, but
not what I was looking for in life - - - I did
something I absolutely did not want to do.
That is exactly what I didn't want to do. I did
not want to obey a bunch of strict rules and
regulations. It was almost like I was willing
to live with moments of happiness along with
moments of hurt and sadness, just so I didn't
have to obey all those commands. I did not
want to live what I perceived to be a very
restricted life.

I wanted freedom to do what I wanted to
do, and not be told what was right and wrong.
I was having too much fun in the world and
did not want to give up that freedom. I did
not want to become a mean-hearted, Bible
thumping, judgmental person. In fact I rather
enjoyed arguing against Christ. It was like I

had an expanded mind and could see beyond the need for a god. Yet, I knew I was missing that deep inner peace.

Jesus Put His Rules In Place To Protect Me

I did want that joy even though I didn't define it as such at the time. So I gave in and decided to begin to lay up for myself treasures in heaven where moth and rust could not destroy and thieves could not break in and steal. I decided to at least try to obey His commands for a while - - - six months. What I discovered was mind boggling. I discovered that Jesus put His commands in place to protect me and give me a better life. He put His commands in place because of His tremendous love for me and not to restrict my life.

I Had Rules For My Children

I had rules for my children as they grew up because I loved them and knew what was best for them. I didn't want them to ride their bikes on busy highways because they could be killed. I didn't want them to hang out with the wrong kids in school because they might pick up some bad habits. I made them eat proper meals so their bodies would become strong and healthy. I encouraged them to study and get their homework done so they would have good enough grades to go on and pursue whatever career they wanted to pursue. My rules for my children may have seemed restrictive at the time, but I set them in place because I loved them and knew what was best for them. I also knew far more about life than they knew.

In the same way Jesus has set some rules in place because He loves us and wants the very best for us. As I knew what was best for my children, Jesus knows what is best for me. He can see what tomorrow will bring when I can't see what the next second will bring. He is able to see what the end result of my disobedience will bring where I can only see the momentary pleasure of the disobedience. So is it wise to obey His commands, or should I take control of my life, having no idea what tomorrow will bring, or what the result of my disobedience will bring? I now realize that obeying His commands is the very best road I can take. I have to admit I am not perfect in obedience, but I do know for the best possible life I need to obey as much as possible. These laws and rules have become my treasure map to finding complete joy as I walk on this earth.

Let's look at parts of the treasure map Jesus has set before us and discover how brilliant He really is. Some of these commands can be found in Matthew, chapters 5-7 and are referred to the as the "Sermon on the Mount". In this section Jesus took some of the Old Testament commands and made them even more strict. He did this to give us a better understanding of why God made the law in the first place. You will note, too, it was done in love and concern for the people around Him.

For example, in Matthew 5:22 Jesus talks about murder. We know it is wrong to murder and most people feel a little self righteous because they have never murdered anyone.

Jesus adds to the command,

"- - - but I tell you that anyone who is angry with his brother will be subject to judgment - - -."

It almost sounds like Jesus is taking this Old Testament command and adding more to it so no one on the face of this earth could ever consider themselves righteous before God. That may be part of it, but I would encourage you to look beyond that thought and gaze right into the heart of this loving Jesus.

At the time Jesus was speaking these words, the religious leaders of the day were so angry at Jesus that they wanted Him dead. They were not willing to kill Him themselves because the people held Jesus in high regard. However, with all that rage in their hearts I wonder how well they slept at night - - - if at all? I wonder how kind they were to their wives, as it is pretty hard to be kind when you are raging inside? I wonder if their children would run and hide in the closet when their raging father came through the door at night? Plus, the emotion of anger can literally cause a body to become ill.

One study from the University of Washington cited that anger in women may be a cause of depression, while uncontrolled anger in men may cause health problems like high blood pressure and an accelerated heart rate. Another study from Ohio State University found that wounds healed slower in a person who had trouble controlling their anger. Plus, children with "anger control issues" have problem-ridden interpersonal relationships as well as greater health problems.

Is it no wonder that Jesus, who loves us so much, wants us to deal with our anger through forgiveness, reconciliation, and prayer? Isn't it interesting that the God who created us, knows what will destroy us, and thus set up a law against that destructive force? That seems to shed a more positive light on obeying the laws. Plus if this anger management law is obeyed we will automatically live a more joy filled life.

I Would Rather Take Control Than Obey

Let me give you a personal example of obeying God's law. This example is not quite as extreme as murder, but to me it was an eye opener. In Proverbs 3: 5-6 God tells us:

"Trust in the Lord with all your heart and lean not on your own understanding; in all your ways acknowledge Him, and He will make your paths straight."

Being a "take control" kind of person, trusting in God and leaning not on my own understanding does not come easy to me. As the sales manager for a twenty state area for adidas I was on the fast track to success. I was climbing the corporate ladder. Nothing was going to get in my way until the day my son climbed into my suitcase.

After two years as sales manager, which consisted of much travel, I realized that to be more successful I would have to travel even more. But my family was young and even though my wife was doing a wonderful job raising our three children, they still needed a father figure in the home.

One day after a tiring trip I got home, opened my suitcase and left it open on the bed. That meant my wife would wash my clothes, repack it, and I would be out the door on another road trip early the next morning.

My four year old had picked up on that routine and asked, "Dad, are you leaving us again in the morning?" Normally his eyes were full of life and excitement, but when I told him yes his whole demeanor changed and he almost cried.

My quick fix was to ask him if he wanted to go with me. Immediately there was fire in his eyes once again , and he almost shouted, "Yes, dad!" So I said, "Okay, Brad, then go and jump in my suitcase." His little legs carried him down the hall as fast as they could, and he jumped up on the bed and jumped into my suitcase.

I didn't think much about it until I returned to my bedroom twenty minutes later and there he was, still sitting in my suitcase - - - chin held high - - - smiling as broad as I have ever seen him smile. It broke my heart. I was successful in business but what was my success doing to my family? Was it edifying my family or tearing it apart? Up to that point I was on a success journey, "leaning on my own understanding."

I knew what the answer had to be. I had to lean on God's understanding because my only understanding and goal was to be successful. My wife and I prayed about it that night and two days later I went into the president's office and resigned as sales manager for adidas. I didn't care what it would cost me, I had to do it.

You see my choice, not knowing how it would affect my family, was to become as successful in my career as I could. God's better choice was for me to become the successful father figure to my three beautiful children.

I couldn't see what my choices would bring down the road, but God could and He corrected me and redirected my path. At that time in my life I trusted in the Lord, chose the unwise direction from a worldly view, and He made my future a whole lot easier to travel. So I ask, "Is God's way restrictive or wise?"

I Even Have To Love My Enemies?

Let me use one more example of why it is wise to obey God by using one of the hardest, if not almost impossible, laws to obey. This law, given by Jesus is found in Matthew 5:43-44. Jesus tells us:

> *"You have heard that it was said, Love your neighbor and hate your enemy. But I tell you: Love your enemies and pray for those who persecute you."*

And I say, "You pray for them, Jesus! You have no idea how deeply they hurt me". Love your enemies and then pray for them? I will have to say this seems ridiculously impossible and, in fact, it is unless you are very close to God Himself.

Let me first of all explain that God never said to hate our enemies. That is something that came into being in the years before Christ. It was a misinterpretation by

67

the rabbis from a Psalm David wrote where he said he hated those who hate the Lord. He said in Psalm 139:22.

"I have nothing but hatred for them; I count them my enemies."

God never gave us the right to hate our enemies but this passage was interpreted to mean that we can hate anyone who disagrees with us, including our religious beliefs.

The word Jesus uses for love here is agape, the highest form of love possible. It is not an emotional type of love. It is a love that says it is my will to love you, no matter what you do to me. It is the way God loves us, and goes way beyond the emotions of loving someone because they are kind and loving to you. Agape love is a love that will never allow any bitterness towards another person to invade our hearts. In fact, it is a love that will only seek the good of the other person no matter how badly they have hurt you.

Why does Jesus tell us to love our enemy this way, and how will it bring us joy if we obey it? I have to search my own heart and ask myself how many times, day and night, I have argued with an enemy who was not even in my presence? How many times have I ranted and raged over someone who has hurt me in some way, and yet they may not even know I am upset with them?

I have even found, as a married man, when I am upset with someone, or my wife is upset with someone, we talk about it on Monday, Tuesday, Wednesday, Thursday, Friday, Saturday, and Sunday and then continue discussing it into the next week or even next month. So I am not the only one upset. Now my wife is upset and neither of us can sleep at night. Then, because we are both upset, our children even experience the moodiness from our anger.

Getting even with our enemies is the more natural path to travel. It is more

69

natural for us to experience anger and rage against our enemy, but that causes us all sorts of physical and emotional ailments. Loving our enemies brings us a tranquility and peace.

Jesus goes on then to help us begin to experience a love for our enemies. He says, "pray for them," and He means pray for their good and pray for their well being. (Do not pray for them to have a tragic car accident.)

Can you imagine how rapidly your emotional state can change if you begin to pray for the well being of your enemy? You might even pray that God would reveal to you where they hurt and why they act the way they do. Maybe they just received a pink slip from work or maybe they were abused as a child in some way. Understanding their hurts would give you a whole lot more compassion towards them.

This command takes a supernatural intervention to obey, and so it will only happen if you are walking close to God. But it will bring you a world of peace in your heart and that is exactly why Jesus wants us to obey this command. Because of His great love for us, His desire for us is to obey His commands so we are able to experience complete joy as we walk on this earth.

The Advantage My Obedience Gives Me

There are many other verses concerning God's commands, and I would challenge you to look them up and discover the wonderful reasons He put them in place. I would challenge you not to look at them as negative commands but as commands given because He loves you. Let me finish this chapter with a little humor from the hundred and nineteenth Psalm. In this Psalm the author is bent on obeying God's commands, statutes, precepts, laws, decrees; and then explains

71

the advantages this obedience brings into his life. Look at the following verses teach us:

> **119:1** *We are blessed when we obey.* I love to be blessed!
>
> **119:32** *They have set my heart free.* It's not a restricted life, it's freedom.
>
> **119:98** *Your commands make me wiser than my enemy.* Now that really excites me!
>
> **119:105** *They help me find the right path.* No more questioning my every move.
>
> **119:111** *They bring joy to my heart.* I love joy!
>
> **119:128** *Teaches me which paths are wrong.* Keeps me out of a lot of trouble.
>
> **119:130** *They give understanding to the simple.* No comment here.
>
> **119:144** *They give me understanding.*

The treasure map to a joy-filled life on this earth leads us to obey God's commands. God's commands are not burdensome, not restrictive, and do not rob us of pleasure on this earth. God's commands simply keep us out of trouble and keep us from destroying our lives and the lives of our loved ones. God's commands were written to give us a better life.

The treasure and the treasure map are in plain sight. The problem is, there are so few who are willing to follow it. It's in plain sight, but so many people walk by it and turn their heads the other way because they do not understand that these commands have love written all over them. "For God so loved the world (me) - - - ". The Psalmist in Psalm 119 states:

"Direct me in the path of your commands, for there I find delight"
Psalm 119:35

Look at one more verse that will prompt you to obey God's commands. It is found in the Old Testament book of Deuteronomy. Moses has led the Israelites out of Egypt and they are now ready to enter the promised land, a beautiful land of milk and honey. Moses told his people in Deuteronomy 4:40

> *"Keep His decrees and commands, which I am giving you today, so that it may go well with you and your children after you and that you may live long in the land the Lord your God gives you for all time".*

That same promise holds today. If I keep God's commands, my children will experience an easier life as they walk on this earth. How many of you desire for your children to experience an easier life, not a "problem free life" just "fewer problems in life"? That promise fills my heart with joy.

But Obeying His Commands Is Not a Treasure Map To Heaven

One final note in this chapter. Obeying God's commands is the treasure map to complete joy on this earth, but it is not the treasure map to heaven. Too many people think that if they do a lot of good deeds (obey God's commands) they will automatically receive a pass into heaven. The Bible does not define and never has defined the pathway to heaven in that way. The Bible tells us we are saved by grace and not by works (not by good deeds) Ephesians 2:8-9.

We are saved because Jesus died on the cross and paid the penalty for our sins. When we go to Him, ask for forgiveness, and ask Jesus to be Lord of our life, to direct us and lead us, that is our ticket to heaven. Obeying Him can only happen after this first step has been made. So, to experience complete joy on this earth you must:

1. Admit you are a sinner.
2. Ask God to forgive you of your sins.
3. Ask Jesus to be Lord of your life.
4. Obey His commands because you know
    He is a whole lot wiser than you are.
5. And begin to experience complete joy.

That is the treasure map to complete joy and a deep inner peace. The map has to be in that order, because it is impossible to obey God's commands unless you have experienced God's forgiveness in your heart. It is impossible to obey God's commands unless you trust that He wants the best for you and that He has your back.

No matter what you think about God's commands or how you perceive them, here is one last verse that delights my heart and keeps me focused on the positive part of obeying God's laws. Joshua 1:8 states:

"Do not let this Book of the law depart from your mouth; meditate on it day and night, so you may be careful to do everything written in it. Then you will be prosperous and successful"

Chapter #5

Is It A Treasure When It Hurts

How can you possibly experience joy while you are going through a crisis? How can you be joyful when you just received a pink slip from work? How can you experience joyful moments after you received divorce papers you had no idea were coming? How can you be joyful when receiving news that one of your children has been seriously hurt or has some awful disease? Is it really possible to be joyful when your world begins to fall apart? The answer is yes, it is. And that is the beauty of joy - - - there is no negative side to counter this emotion. Let me share a couple experiences in my life to drive this point home.

Our Oldest Son Had Black And Blue Marks All Over His Body

I discovered this fact during a very difficult time in my life. One day our oldest son, at the age of five, had large black and blue marks all over his body. I seriously wondered if Beverly had been beating him, though she had no history of abuse. In fact, my wife is a very mild tempered woman.

She set up a doctor's appointment and got in the next day. I called home that evening and asked what the doctor had discovered. She asked if I was sitting down and then told me the doctor said our son was bleeding internally, and that it looked like he had leukemia. Then she dropped the big bomb that he might only have two or three days to live. The doctor wanted to keep him in the hospital, but my wife insisted on bringing him home to spend as much time with him as possible.

Talk about an emotional downer. I excused myself from the dinner with my clients and began the long one hour drive home. It didn't take me long to begin telling God what I thought of Him. I started out reminding Him about all the things I was doing for Him, and how I had decided to go into the ministry --- and He allows something like this to happen? I told Him I wasn't sure I even wanted to follow Him if this was all the protection He provided.

Then I began calling Him a few names I probably shouldn't have called Him and demanded that He put an end to this awful scenario. I went on like this for half an hour, shaking my fist at Him and screaming out my venom towards Him. Finally I came to a point where I could only cry because I was emotionally and physically exhausted.

At that point God began to gently put some beautiful thoughts in my mind. Thoughts like:

- *Can't I teach your son to play T-ball better than you can?*
  - - - I answered, "Yes, God, You can."
- *Can't I teach your son more about back packing than you can?*
  - - - again, "Yes, God, You can."
- *Can't I be a better father to your son than you can?*
  - - - "Yes, God, You can."
- Then I heard something that broke my heart and yet brought me comfort at the same time when He said,

  "OK then, give him to Me."

At that point I emotionally lifted my son up and gave him to God. There were tears in my eyes but I was at total peace with what God was asking me to do. I even had a moment of joy as I pictured my beautiful son walking hand in hand with this all powerful

God who loved him far more than I ever could, a God who would protect my son from all the hurts he would experience on this earth.

Is there a treasure even when you hurt? Yes, there is. I have witnessed joy at one of the lowest points in my life. It came to me in the form of a "deep inner peace", a peace that God loves me and my son and that even the worst scenario I could imagine could not take that peace and that joy away. As a footnote, my son is now 36 and has a beautiful family of his own. He was allergic to sulfa, which was in a medicine he was taking. When he came home we saw no need to give it to him anymore. Talk about a miracle!

Joy May Not Be Immediate

As I share this next example of joy during hurtful times I will have to admit that joy was not an immediate emotion. My wife and I struggled during this crisis and the joy did not come till later. We had announced we were going into the ministry and my 15 year old daughter reacted in a less than excited manner. Sha (Long A), our first born, has always been a beautiful daughter and normally well behaved, but this news did not please her one little bit. Then, on top of this heart wrenching news, we planned to move her from a small school she had attended all her life to a huge school in her junior year. She had no friends and it was like we had ruined her life. Sha began to rebel.

Beverly and I began to pray intently for her. Nothing happened. We prayed even harder and still nothing happened. We were sure God had called us into the ministry and even that He had called us to this new town to take on our first church. But we were struggling because He had apparently forgotten to include our daughter in the call. One year of prayer went by and then another. She graduated very high in her class but it was like we had lost our daughter. Then on to college which exposed her to a whole new world of freedom.

We prayed even harder that God would touch her heart and draw her back into His arms. Nothing happened! She didn't become a terrible person during this time. She was simply experiencing more life than we wanted her to experience. But we kept praying and then prayed some more. During this time she was dating nice boys, but we knew they were not boys that would make her a pleasing husband. Where was God during this six year period? Was He even listening to our prayers and petitions?

Then, just before graduation, something special happened in her life. Because of our prayers and the prayers of a special friend, Sha got to know a godly young man from Oregon. They had never even met but communicated through writing. Four months later, after meeting on only two separate occasions, they were married. God was working in this situation for six years. We just didn't see it.

As a follow up to that situation, Sha called us a few years later and asked for us to pray about her husband being called into the ministry. Just a little setback because of the trouble we had when we were called into the ministry, I asked her if she wanted us to pray for it or against it? She said, without hesitation, "Please pray for it." I chuckled as I prayed thinking - - - prayer is powerful, and doesn't God have a wonderful sense of humor? She hated it with such a passion and now she wants to become a pastor's wife. So yes, you can experience joy on this earth even during your most difficult times.

And Now --- Even Our Third Child Was Affected

Another difficult family time came the day we announced to our family that we were being called into the ministry at my mother's birthday party. We went home that evening and while wrestling with my three year old son I noticed that he was a little more clumsy than usual. I also noticed that his right eye was turning in ever so slightly.

I put my hand over the other eye and he quickly pulled it away and asked me not to turn out the lights. On the day we announced that we were going into the ministry I realized that my son had lost total sight in his right eye. How could God allow this to happen? The next day we took him to the eye doctor and he diagnosed it as possibly being retinolblastoma (cancer).

Being a fairly new Christian and having a boatload of faith we took him to the altar the next Sunday and had him anointed with oil and prayed over. Nothing happened and to this day (31 years later) he is still blind in his right eye. Where was God in all this? Why did God allow me to discover this tragedy the day we announced we were going into the ministry?

Fortunately it was not cancer, but was later diagnosed as Coats disease (a totally detached retina). Still, why would God allow this to happen? Now my son was handicapped or at least I thought so. But why hadn't God answered our prayers? About twenty years later I realized that God had answered our prayers. He had touched my son in a miraculous way but not the way I asked.

People who have only one eye have no depth perception and thus have trouble measuring distance. John had perfect depth perception with only one eye. He was one of the best outfielders on our church softball team, requiring almost perfect depth perception. Later John played backup goalie on a college soccer team. With balls coming at him at 70 mph from ten feet away he had to have amazing depth perception. God had answered our prayers, just in a different way than we asked. He always answers the prayers of those who follow Him!

Some may argue here, that God answered all our prayers but that we have never had to go through the loss of a child. You are right, but with our oldest son we were willing to lay him in the arms of our God and still have that deep inner peace. So, though we have never had to go through that terrible loss; emotionally, we felt much of the pain.

Are you able to experience joy even during the toughest times in your life? Are you able to experience joy even when your world seems to be falling apart? The answer is yes. The apostle Paul experienced it while in a Roman prison chained between two hardened Roman soldiers. In fact, he wrote the most joy-filled book in the Bible (Philippians) during that time.

We had that deep inner peace when we thought we were going to lose our son, and when our daughter rebelled as we went into the ministry, and when our son went blind in one eye as a little boy. Yes, joy will always be with you even during the saddest of times if you follow the treasure map in the previous chapter.

But how is that possible, you ask? The next chapter will help you understand the way. It's so simple, and it doesn't cost you a cent. Interested?

Chapter #6

Protecting The Treasure

Isn't it sad to see someone win a lottery and then within the first two years declare bankruptcy? How can someone win five million dollars and be broke in two years? It's because they drain their winnings by thinking they have an inexhaustible amount of money. They go on a spending spree and purchase a lot of toys, trips, and entertainment. They spend, spend, spend, and then spend some more until their winnings are totally gone. They do not protect their treasure.

Wouldn't it be wiser to go to an outside financial advisor and get some advice from someone who knows how to handle money? They could possibly spend $500,000 or even $1,000,000 on a new home and a few toys but then invest the rest and after the spending spree is over live on the interest from the investment for the rest of their lives.

In the same way it is sad when a person finds spiritual joy, that deep inner peace, and then just lives on that one day high until it seems to get weaker and weaker and then vanishes. Recently I had a hip replacement and even while in the recovery room I was in a euphoric state of mind. Everything was wonderful. The surgery was a great success, and I was even up and walking that same evening.

It was exciting to be in the hospital. It was exciting to go home a day early because I was doing so well. But then, a few weeks later, I realized my excitement and euphoria existed because of the pain medication I was on. It was wonderful until I had to start decreasing it. Then the highs were not so high and the excitement started to decrease. And finally one day I stopped taking it all together. The high was wonderful while it lasted but it began to wear off quickly.

The same will be true with the joy you discover as you ask Jesus to be Lord of your life. It is wonderful. It is like a high. But if you don't continue to protect it, it too will wane. In fact Andre Crouch wrote a song titled "Take Me Back" and one of the lines was, "Take me back to the place I first believed." In other words Andre Crouch is saying that the spiritual high was wonderful while it lasted but it just didn't last forever. It didn't last because it was not protected.

So how do we protect this new found joy in our lives? How do we protect this deep inner peace that is so beautiful and so fulfilling? Once again the answer is simple, it just takes a little energy and a little work. This is where the book will end for many readers, because many will agree that these next two directives are good but they will never plug them into their lifestyle. I am going to spell out two ways to protect that new found joy and deep inner peace. Neither of these exercises can be neglected if we desire to continue on this wonderful new path.

#1 - By Continually Reminding Ourselves Of God's Love And Goodness

First, we can only maintain that joy when we continually remind ourselves of the glory of our God, that He truly loves us and only wants the very best for us. If we can plug that into our understanding, it's like protecting that joy every day we are alive.

Here is how that works. We continually look into God's Word and find verses that support the fact that God is glorious, that He does love us deeply, and that He only wants the very best for our lives. Then we memorize these verses and during the times we feel our joy is waning, we recall them and remember the wonder of the God we serve. We have a plaque on our wall that states, "Just when you feel that God is all you have - - - that's when you realize He is all you need."

Let's look at just a few of the encouraging verses that protect our deep inner peace. There are enough to write another book about, but we will only look at a few. I would encourage you, however, to set up your own library of God's loving and guiding desires for us.

John 3:16 is a verse that almost every Christian has memorized at one time or another. It even seems to show up at a lot of football games. It is ever before us but do we, as Christians, take time to understand the beauty of this verse?

For God Loves Me So Much

It starts out, "For God so loved the world." I am a part of the world and a person created in God's image so the verse could accurately be translated, "For God loved me so much - - - ." God created me in His image so He could pour out His love upon me, so He could immerse me in His love. That alone could draw me back to that deep inner peace during a trying time. This great all-knowing God loves me in spite of my many failures and shortcomings. And then the verse goes on to reveal the unbearable action He took so that I could be in His presence forever and ever. He wanted to assure Himself that He would never have to let go of me so He had His own Son die on the cross and pay the penalty for my sins.

When I am feeling unhappy, all I need to do is reinvest my joy by meditating on that fact. God loves me, even though I am often unlovable and sinful and even though I have been known to break His heart. He still loves me! No matter how sorrowful I become or how much I physically hurt, I just need to be aware of God's perfect love for me. That is called protecting my joy.

Plans To Prosper Me And Give Me Hope

Along that same line look what God states in Jeremiah 29:11,

> *"For I know the plans I have for you declares the Lord, plans to prosper you and not harm you, plans to give you hope and a future".*

It is so wise to protect your joy by knowing this verse. There will be times in your life when you won't be able to sense God's presence. It may seem like He has no interest in you because He is not answering your prayers. You may even feel like He is not revealing to you the direction He wants you to go. When these doubts come just say Jeremiah 29:11 from memory. It will bring sunshine back into your life for He plans to prosper you, give you hope and a future.

When going through a valley (often brought on by your own bad decisions) God desires to prosper you and give you hope (not discouragement) and a future. I cannot say it enough, God wants the very best for His children - - - always. So instead of grumbling and having insecure thoughts about God, you need to protect your joy (re-up your joy) by grabbing hold of this verse and believing every single word of it. God only wants to prosper you (spiritually) and give you hope and a beautiful future.

The very first verse I memorized as a Christian was Romans 8:28. The verse just overwhelmed me because I couldn't believe that God could take my mistakes and turn them into something positive. I have trouble believing that God can take difficult situations I have with other people and turn them into something good. But Romans 8:28 says,

"And we know that in all things God works for the good of those who love Him - - -".

Now that verse is able to re-up my joy even in the most difficult of times. Knowing that verse will always protect my joy. The promise is, "God can make every incident in my life (bad or good) turn into something good" and the condition is "if I truly love Him and am willing to serve Him whole-heartedly".

One other verse that many Christians have difficulty with is Proverbs 3:9-10. It states:

"Honor the Lord with your wealth, with the first fruits of your crops; then your barns will be filled to overflowing, and your vats will brim over with new wine"

A more modern translation of that

verse would be, "Give back to God 10% of everything you make and He, in turn, will give you an abundance of everything you will need as you live on this earth. He will supply every need you have and will give you so much extra it will overflow your bank account." If I give, God will provide. Most people don't trust God to hold up His end of that promise so they don't hold up theirs. They do not meet the condition and miss out on the joy.

These verses will help you protect your deep inner peace. They will help you see that God will always be with you and that He only wants to bless you, not with just spiritual blessings, but with earthly things as well. Make yourself familiar with verses that reveal to you His glory and love and purpose and you will be on your way to protecting your joy, your deep inner peace.

#2 - *God Was With You Then And Is Still With You*

But the second exercise is every bit as important. In order to protect your joy you must also go through some of life's difficult circumstances. God was with you then, and He will guide you and sustain you through all future events.

When I thought my son was going to die of leukemia, even before I knew the outcome, God gave me the joy in knowing He could give the son I loved so much a greater life than I could. He was with me through one of the most difficult situations in my life and I have to remind myself that He will be with me, encouraging me and guiding me, in every future situation I feel I can not get through.

It's so interesting that every new difficult situation seems insurmountable. It's like God is not with me, not listening to my plea, and not answering my prayers. But as I look back over my life at the difficulties I have endured, I know He was with me then, and He will not let me down now. I know it! I know it! I know it!

Why Was My Brother Killed?

What are some of the hard times in your life you thought you could not possibly endure, but now as you look back on them you see the hand of God "working everything together for your good"? My brother, Joel, the youngest of six, was killed in a construction accident at the age of 20. He was a delightful boy and one whom everyone enjoyed. He was not a good football player because he was too kind hearted. Why did he have to die so young while rapists and killers remained alive?

We were raised in a Christian home and were fairly good people in our community (though I wandered away for over thirteen years). But as Joel began to wander, was it possible that God knew he would wander so far he would never come back? By taking Joel from this earth was God saying He was not willing to lose my brother? Was God saying He loved Joel far too much to let go of him for all eternity? I do not know the exact answer here, but I trust God and that thought helped me see the intense loving character of the God I serve with delight.

Can you look back and see the hand of God in your most difficult situations? I hope you can because seeing that will help you protect your joy and deep inner peace. It will help you see the true character of the God you serve or are about to serve. My wife and I have just read about how God miraculously delivered the Israelites from the hand of the Pharaoh in Egypt. You talk about power and might and concern for His people. Yet we serve the same powerful, loving, gracious, and concerned God today. He is no different.

He has not changed in the last 5000 years. He does not love you any less than He loved them. You are praying to that same God today - - - the same exact God.

These are the two most important steps in protecting your treasure;

#1 Continually remind yourself of God's love and goodness by memorizing verses that support these truths.

#2 Remember that God was with you during your most difficult times in life and he will continue to be with you in the future.

Is the treasure great enough that you are willing to work at keeping it or is this simply too much work? That is a question only you are able to answer. The right answer will protect your joy and even multiply it as you grow older. The wrong answer will cause your joy to fade and you, too, will begin singing, "take me back to the time I first believed."

Epilogue

This is a book that has been on my heart for seven years and by reading it you may come to the conclusion that I have my life all together and that I am always joyful. That is just not true. I am usually very upbeat, and I love to laugh but there are times I want to scream out, "Where are you God? Can't you do something about my situation?" Then for a moment my joy might escape me.

To me, the contents in this book point toward a journey and not a conclusion. A journey is traveled one step at a time. Your first step may be asking God to forgive you of your sins and inviting Jesus to be Lord of your life. I thought I was a Christian all through high school because I was a good person and went to church four times on Sunday.

I remember reading the Bible during that time, and it was somewhat boring. I studied it for a Bible quiz team, but all I did was memorize it and never really let it touch my heart. Later, after my conversion, I could not put the book down. Every word seemed to warm my heart. So maybe your first step to joy is allowing Jesus to be Lord of your life.

Perhaps you have sincerely taken that step and have patterned your life to be like His. If that is the case your next step may be to begin looking for passages in the Bible that help you see how very special you are in God's sight and how much He loves you. Roman 5:8 may be a start.

"But God demonstrates His own love for us in this: While we were still sinners (enemies of God), Christ died for us." (parenthesis added)

While I was still an enemy of God, living a self centered life, using language that broke His heart, shaking my fist at Him in anger, God, in love, sent His son to die on the cross and pay the penalty for my sins. Now that is LOVE! Are you able to accept that much love? Most of us feel unworthy of that love and even as Christians go around feeling that God is always disappointed with us. Get over it! God loves you even in your imperfection.

You might be at a point on your journey where you know about His love, but you have never taken time to connect that love to your life and it's time you did so. That is when you look back over your life and see where He has lovingly touched you and brought you through troubled times. Those times have helped develop you into what you are today. My embarrassment over being poor encouraged me to begin earning a lot of money which helped me see how unfulfilling money really is.

Many Christians who truly love the Lord have never shared their joyful journey with a neighbor or fellow worker. That may be the next step on the journey. They have never encouraged someone to know Jesus themselves. Thus, they have never seen a life truly transformed. Their life was drastically changed yet they have never encouraged another life to be drastically changed. That's like keeping refreshing drinking water in a stagnant pond.

Gradually it becomes undrinkable and then evaporates away. The joy in the hearts of many Christians has become stagnant and then even evaporated, leaving a hard shell of a Christian who is not a lot of fun to be around.

Yes, Jesus does want us to know His joy so that our joy may be complete. But we will likely never know that complete joy while still on this earth because of our sinful nature and the exposure we have to sin and deceit. Yet we are able to travel towards that end by beginning the journey wherever we are right now. It's not rocket science, it is just a willingness to begin.

God Will Put On Your Heart Any Changes He Wants You To Make

As a final example of that journey let me share one more personal experience with you. Maybe God desires to give you a refreshing and new direction in your life and you are afraid of that direction. After my conversion in that brand new, all paid for, Mercedes Benz, I simply could not get enough of God's Holy Word. Every word came alive and just jumped off the page and into my heart. I began to see the wisdom and love and beauty in the life that God had for me.

My life changed drastically and I wanted to share my changes with every one around me. At the time I was a sales representative for adidas, a job any athletic minded person would kill for. I was meeting with some of the most upbeat and exciting business men and women in Michigan and even some of the pro athletes. I loved sales and I loved being able to travel every day to a different location.

Yet, I just wanted to share God's Word and see lives changed like mine was changed. Since I had an outgoing personality, loved to be up front in a crowd, and loved to share God's Word, the next step in my journey was to become a pastor. Too many people are afraid that if they fully surrender to God they will have to become a missionary or preacher or weird, street corner, Jesus freak.

That is absolutely not true. God considered my giftedness and led me in a new direction that would bring me even more satisfaction than selling athletic shoes. God will consider your giftedness, your passion, and abilities and then direct you toward something that will bring you a greater joy. As He touched my heart, all I could dream about was sharing His Word. My sales job was wonderful but I had a hard time concentrating on it as my mind was off in another direction.

I share this example with you to help you see you never have to be afraid of your future when you walk with the Lord. He will lead you into experiences that will start you on your journey to JOY, and it will be exciting. Are you ready? Pack your backpack if you are and simply let go of your self centered journey. Then, let the journey begin.